W9-CII-883

Looking Good

DECORATING YOUR ROOM

by Arlene C. Rourke

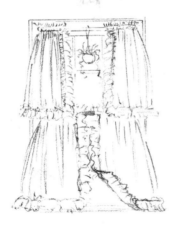

Rourke Publications, Inc.
Vero Beach, FL 32964

The author wishes to thank **Eileen Griffin** for her work on the illustrations in this book. Ms. Griffin is an artist, illustrator and the owner of a graphic arts company.

© 1989 Rourke Publications, Inc.

Library of Congress Cataloging-in-Publication Data

Rourke, Arlene C., 1944-
    Decorating you room / by Arlene C. Rourke.

      p.   cm. — (Looking good)
    Includes index.
    Summary: Advice for decorating your bedroom, with tips on style, color, lighting, furniture, window treatment, and floors.
    1. Bedrooms—Juvenile literature. 2. Interior decoration— Juvenile literature. [1. Bedrooms. 2. Interior decoration.] I. Title. II. Series: Looking good (Vero Beach, Fla.)
NK2117.B4R68   1989   88-38500
747.7'7—dc 19   CIP
ISBN 0-86625-286-X   AC

CONTENTS

YOUR ROOM

Your room is your private haven. You can go into your room, close the door on the world, and just be alone for a while — thinking, dreaming, sleeping, or working. Your room reflects your ideas, your personality, even your fantasies. Your room isn't exactly like anyone else's room because you aren't exactly like anyone else.

If you're thinking of redecorating your room, you'll want to assess your needs, your wants, and your style. What *is* your style? Are you the girl next door in jeans and a ponytail (casual), or a city slicker (modern high tech), or a romantic in lace (Victorian). Have a mental picture of the style you want in your room before you begin to decorate.

YOUR STRATEGY

Taking Inventory

Beautiful rooms don't just happen; they're planned. Before you go out and buy one gallon of paint, plan your strategy. The first thing to do is take inventory. Get a piece of paper and start writing. What do you already have and what do you need to get? A bed. Twin size. Do you share a room with your sister? Two twin beds. Dressers, chairs and desks. What else? Lamps? Don't worry about the smaller concerns, like throw pillows, let's just concentrate on the major pieces for now.

Taking Accurate Measurements

Seeing your room on graph paper can make decorating a lot easier. Using a piece of graph paper, make a floor plan of your room. Let's say that a ½" square is equal to one foot. That means that a room measuring 10' x 16' will be 5" x 8". If you use standard size graph paper a box measures ¼". Most rooms have some unusual architectural feature — a bay window or a fireplace, for instance. Remember to include them in your plan. Don't forget windows and doors, being careful to indicate which way the door opens.

Now measure every stick of furniture in your room. Measure the height, width, and depth. Take careful notes. If your measurements are off your plan will be inaccurate.

> **TIP:** If you want to be really scientific about your room plan, you can buy a kit which will provide the graph paper as well as specially sized pieces of furniture which can be moved around until you have the arrangement you like.

If you'd rather spend your money on the actual decoration, you can always make furniture cut-outs. Remember to keep them in the correct size (½"=1'). Use your graph and cut-outs to rearrange the furniture, making the most of the room's space and the architectural features. We'll go further into furniture placement later but, by now, you should have a good idea of what you need and where you want it placed.

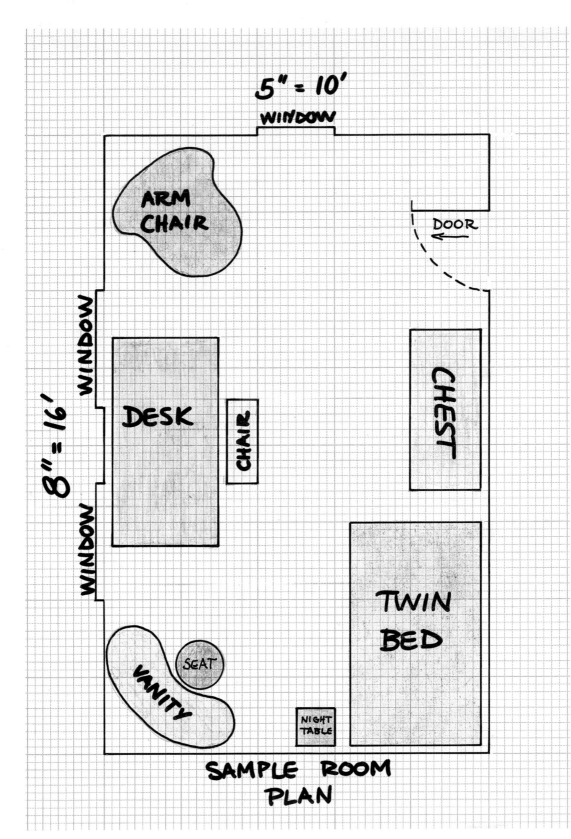

5" = 10'

WINDOW

ARM CHAIR

DOOR

WINDOW

8" = 16'

DESK

CHAIR

CHEST

WINDOW

VANITY

SEAT

NIGHT TABLE

TWIN BED

SAMPLE ROOM PLAN

A Word About The Relatives

Any plans you have for a major overhaul of your room should be discussed fully with your parents. They pay the rent and they like to be consulted about these things. Having decorated a few rooms themselves, they may come up with some good ideas of their own.

You'll need to discuss money. Decorating can be expensive. How big a project will this be? How much money can they spend? Are you going to buy all new furniture or would it be better to strip and refinish the furniture you already have.

At this time Grandma's attic or Aunt Sarah's basement may come into play. Some people are natural pack rats, accumulating all sorts of things over the years. You might want to politely ask these two lovely ladies if you can have a piece that they are not using. If they have something you need, and are willing to part with it, you may be able to save quite a bit of money. Only take what you can use. Remember to say "Thank you."

ELEMENTS OF STYLE

By now you have a good idea of what you have to work with — what pieces of furniture you are keeping, what you have to buy, and how much money you have to spend. Last, but not least, you have the seed of an idea for your dream room. Now you have to make that seed bloom.

Like people, rooms have personality. Some rooms are warm and cozy; they invite you to come in, kick your shoes off, and relax for a while. Other rooms are cold and forbidding; they seem to say, "Don't touch." Let's figure out why some rooms are appealing and some aren't.

Interior decorators agree that all rooms, no matter what their function, incorporate certain elements of style. When these elements are mixed in just the right way, you've got a great room.

Unity is the total effect produced when all elements in the room are seen together as a whole. When you enter a room you are immediately aware of its color, furnishings, carpeting, window treatments, wall decorations, etc. Your eye moves from one object to the other with no sudden stops or quirky jumps. When everything "belongs" with everything else there is an easy flow to a room. That sense of belonging is unity.

Every wall and piece of furniture has a **line**. Not only does a line define the edge of a piece, but it also has a psychological effect. **Vertical lines** give a feeling of strength and stability. They make a room appear higher. Vertical lines are used in formal rooms in the form of tall columns, high fireplaces, and long, heavy drapery.

Horizontal lines are frequently used in modern architecture and design. They give a near-to-the-ground, close-to-nature feel. Horizontal lines give the effect of peace and serenity.

Diagonal lines can produce some really dazzling effects. They induce a feeling of movement and restlessness. Diagonals force the eye to look at something by pointing right to it. When using diagonals, be sure that you're drawing the viewer's eye to something attractive. Another thing to remember about diagonals: they tend to dominate all other lines. Control any urge you may have to use them all over your walls.

Curved lines are graceful and feminine. They give an air of lightness and fun to a room. Here again, a little goes a long way. When overdone, curves can be frantic and cutesy.

10

Out of Scale

In Proper Scale

Scale and **balance** deal with the proportion of one object in relation to the size of the room and the size of the other objects in the room. For instance, a huge, dark four poster bed in a tiny bedroom is out of proportion. It hogs most of the space and leaves little room for other needed furniture. It throws off the unity of the room.

Symmetry

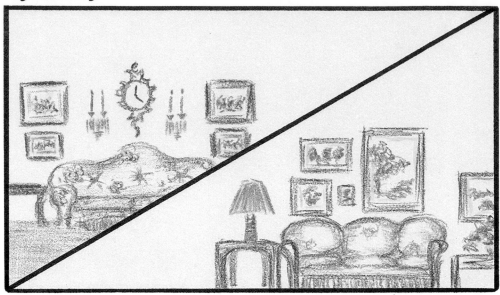

Asymmetry

When all the objects on one side of the room are exactly repeated on the other side of the room, that's called **symmetry. Symmetrical** rooms are usually formal and tend to be a touch stuffy. You'll probably go for an **asymmetrical** look. In an asymmetrical room the objects are of equal size and weight, but they're not identical. They're carefully placed so that no part of the room is "heavier" because it holds most of the furniture.

Sometimes you hear interior decorators using the words **focal point**. A focal point is a feature which immediately draws your eyes to it. Sometimes it's an unusual architectural detail, like a fireplace or a bay window. If you have a focal point in your room, you might want to arrange your design to emphasize it. Not all eyecatching details are attractive. Some features, like an ugly, old radiator, will have to be disguised. Don't worry if your room doesn't have an attractive focal point. You can always create one with an area rug, a poster collection, or some of your own artwork.

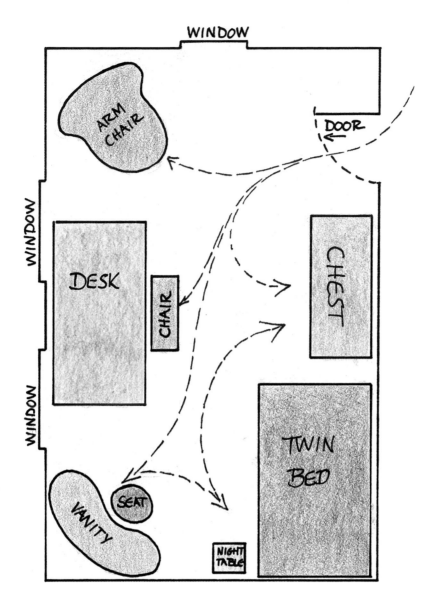

Traffic Patterns

When planning furniture placement, always be aware of **traffic patterns**. As the words imply, traffic patterns are those paths you use everyday to move around in your room. You have a traffic pattern from the bathroom to your bed, from your bed to your dresser, from your dresser to your desk. These lanes should be clear of junk and easy to walk through. Generally speaking, a traffic pattern is at least two feet wide.

COLOR

When decorating your room, choose a color first. Just the thought of picking a color for those big, bare walls is enough to drive some people up the wall. Afraid of trying something new, they stick with the same old boring off-white. Why not add a little zing to your room? **Color is your most powerful decorating tool — don't throw it away**. Choosing colors is a science and can be confusing for a beginner. Knowing the language may help you sort things out.

Hue is the name of a color. It is the purest example of that color, with no other color added. Add white to a hue and you get a **tint**. Add black to that tint and you get a **shade**. For example, red is a hue. Add white to red and you get a pink tint. Add black to that pink tint and you get a shade of dusty rose.

Value has to do with the lightness or darkness of a color. Pink has a lighter value than red.

Intensity is the brightness or dullness of a color. Shocking pink is very bright and really grabs the eye. Dusty rose, while still a pink, is restful and soothing.

The Psychology of Color

Color is usually the first element you notice when you enter a room. Color sets the tone. It evokes an immediate emotional response. **Red** gives a room pizzazz and energy. Most people have a strong emotional response to red. A word of caution: a little red goes a long way. You might want to use a pink tint and save the red for accent. **Blue** and **green** are favorite

Warm Colors

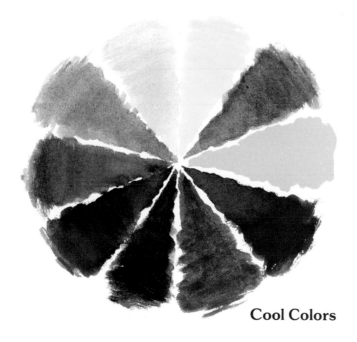

Cool Colors

bedroom colors because they are cool and restful. They evoke images of nature: peaceful, blue skies and tranquil, green forests. **Yellow** is bright and sunny. **Tan** and **off-white**

Monochromatic Colors

Analogous Colors

Contrasting Colors

are classic colors which go well with just about any other color. Mixed with a touch of red, shades in the brown family can be warm and cozy. **Purple** is a color favored by many artists. There's something a little rebellious about purple. In its pure state, purple is too dark for most rooms. Mixed with white it becomes lavender, which is a lovely color for a bedroom.

Moving Colors Around

Even though you've chosen your primary color carefully, you don't want everything in the room to be that exact shade. You'll want to vary your color scheme to create interest. The simplest way to vary color is by using different tints and shades of the same color — for example, brown, tan, and ecru. This is called a **monochromatic design**, and it's the easiest to handle if you're timid about color.

The more adventurous might use an **analagous design**. Analagous colors are three or more hues which are right next to each other on the color wheel — for example, orange, yellow, and green.

A **contrasting design** employs two opposite colors — for example, purple and yellow. Contrasting colors can bring excitement to a room. However, they can be tricky to work with. Be sure that you've considered how *all* the elements in your room will look when seen together.

Light and Color

When choosing color, don't forget to consider the effect that light has on color. The part of the country in which you live or the direction in which your room faces has a lot to do with the tricks light plays with color. Different moods are created by evening light and daylight, as well. Get some paint chips and hold them up to the source of natural light in your room. Check your chips at various times of the day before you decide on a color.

Wall Coverings

Paint is by far the most common wall covering. It's easy to apply, easy to decorate over, and inexpensive. **Latex** paint is water-based, easy to use, dries quickly and cleans with soap and water. **Oil-based** paint is tricky to handle and harder to clean. It's popular in bathrooms because it can be scrubbed. Generally, people use **flat** (matte) paint on walls and **enamel** (glossy) paint on moldings.

> **TIP:** Glossy paint calls attention to anything it covers. If your moldings are not up to inspection it's best to paint them the same color as the walls.

You can achieve some dazzling effects with **wallpaper.** It can add visual interest through pattern and texture. When choosing a pattern, remember what we said about line and color. A word of caution: wallpaper is difficult to put up *and* take down. Before you choose a paper, make sure you really like it and it suits your room. You're going to be living with it for a long time.

FURNITURE

If you're lucky enough to be getting new furniture, make your selection carefully. Furniture is expensive and has to last for years. Start an "ideas file." If the furniture in a picture in a magazine or newspaper appeals to you, cut it out and save it. Furniture manufacturers sometimes offer free catalogues. Check out the public library for decorating books. Visit model homes; they're usually well done because they're professionally decorated.

Generally, it's smarter to choose good furniture with simple, clean lines. This type of furniture goes with everything and grows with you. As you grow your style will change. The cutesy Victorian canopy bed you adored as an eight-year-old may seem "childish" in your teens.

> **TIP:** If you really can't resist the urge for ruffles and lace, splurge on the accessories. Sheets, curtains, and throw pillows are a lot less expensive to change than furniture.

If you can't afford new furniture but your old furniture looks awful, try refinishing it. This could be a fun project for the whole family. Buy a furniture stripping kit and follow the directions. After you've taken the old surface off, smooth over the rough edges and start fresh. You can either stain it or paint it. Remember what we said about monochromatic, analagous and contrasting colors. If you want to be really creative, get a stencil and paint designs onto your furniture. You'll get a personal, one-of-a-kind look.

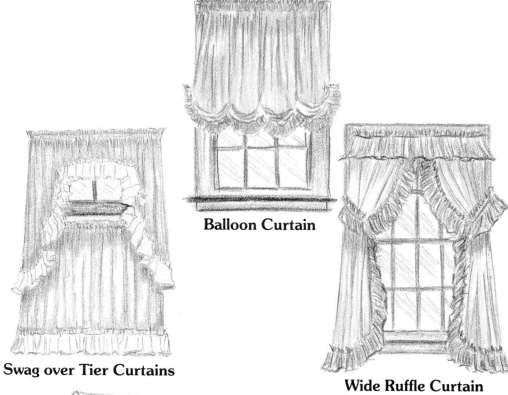

Balloon Curtain

Swag over Tier Curtains

Wide Ruffle Curtain

Lace Window Shade

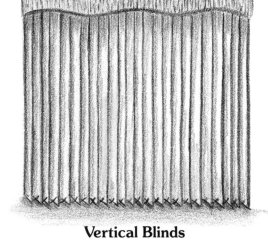

Vertical Blinds

20

WINDOWS

When selecting window treatments, consider the practical aspects first. How much natural light does your room get? Do you need to have your room pitch black in order to sleep? What size are your windows and how many are there? How's the view? How much privacy do you need?

Curtains are one of the most popular window treatments because they are so versatile. They can be made in a wide variety of fabrics and styles to suit any room. Gauzy sheers lend a soft, feminine touch and allow light to enter. If you need privacy or want to make a more modern fashion statement, go for a heavier fabric without pleats or gathers. Never underestimate the power of the lowly sheet. Sheets make wonderful, inexpensive window coverings and tablecloths.

TIP: If you know how to sew, you can save about fifty percent on the cost of curtains by making your own.

Shades are inexpensive and require little care. If you can't find the right shade, try making your own. Completely cover a simple, white pull down shade with the same wallpaper you used on your walls. This is especially effective in a small room. On the other hand, if your wallpaper pattern is too "busy," take the dominant color and use it as a solid color on the shade. Precise measurements are important.

If you can't sleep unless the room is totally dark, you could use a heavy, opaque shade. A lighter weight shade can be used to great effect in a very feminine bedroom. Just cover it with a lacy adhesive fabric. This will give you the look of lace but with more privacy than a lace curtain.

Blinds are less versatile than curtains or shades and are usually harder to install. Mini blinds come in a variety of colors and can add drama to your room. They provide better insulation against winter's cold and summer's heat than curtains or shades. If your windows are standard size, you can buy them ready made. If not, you'll have to have them custom ordered and that can be expensive.

Matchstick blinds look like blinds, but roll up from the bottom like shades. They're cheaper and less formal than blinds and, because they're made of wood, you can paint your own designs on them. No matter how they are pulled there's always a space between the slats. For that reason they don't darken a room well or provide total privacy.

If you have badly shaped windows, try hiding them with **shutters.** Shutters are usually made of wood and can be painted or stained any color.

Since you're going to be reading and studying in your room, it's important that you provide good lighting. During the day your primary source of light is the sun. For the nighttime, you should have enough lamps to provide a balanced pattern of light throughout the room. Be sure you have a good reading light at your desk and your bedside, if you read in bed.

> **TIP:** Colored bulbs produce interesting design effects. A pink bulb gives a bedroom a soft, cozy glow.

FLOORS

When thinking about floor coverings, don't immediately go for the most obvious — wall-to-wall carpeting. Explore all the possibilities — tile, wood, stone, rugs, etc. Take advantage of the materials at hand. If you live in a part of the country where tile or wood is relatively inexpensive, consider using it.

Tile, brick and **slate** are long wearing and easy to clean. Spills can simply be mopped up. **Wood** floors give a room a wonderful warm, solid feeling. Wood is durable and can be painted or stained to achieve a variety of effects. An occasional buffing is all that's necessary to keep it shiny.

For a softer look, carpeting is the answer. **Wall-to-wall carpeting** unifies a room with one unbroken area of color. It is quieter, warmer, and easier on the feet than hard floors.

You might want to use an **area rug** as an accent piece on a hard floor. Because area rugs cover less space than wall-to-wall carpeting, you can go a little wilder with them in color and design. Area rugs are great for unifying and separating different parts of a room. Let's say that you have a special place in your room where you lounge around and talk with friends. A grouping of chairs with an area rug sets this place apart from the rest of the room.

Light colored rugs soil easily and will have to be cleaned more frequently. Some area rugs must be dry cleaned while others, like dhurries, may be washed. Turn your rug every few months so it doesn't get worn in one spot.

FINISHING TOUCHES AND HELPFUL HINTS

Help, My Room Is Too . . .

Small. This is the most common complaint. Use tints of cool colors (blue and green) on the walls. Cool colors tend to recede, making the room look larger. Choose light colored, small-scaled furniture. Avoid a choppy look by placing furniture against the walls. Stay away from heavy drapes on windows. Keep window treatments in the same color family as the walls. Use wall-to-wall carpeting to create a unified look. Wall mirrors can give the illusion of greater space.

Narrow. If your room looks like a railroad car, you'll have to make the longer walls appear shorter and the shorter walls appear longer. Paint the shorter walls a bright color and the longer walls a quieter color. The bright walls will catch the eye and seem larger. Place the headboard of your bed against one of the longer walls. That will divide the space and give the illusion of a shorter wall.

Dark. Paint the walls one of the bright colors, like yellow, light orange, or light green. Select light colored furniture and window treatments which allow the maximum amount of sunlight to enter.

Low. Some older houses were built with low ceilings in order to preserve the heat in winter. Keep your ceiling color white or a very pale tint. Strong vertical lines give the impression of a higher ceiling.

High. High ceilings can give a room a wonderful feeling

of airiness. However, if your ceiling is so high that it throws the rest of the room out of proportion, consider a few adjustments in your color scheme. Paint the ceiling a darker shade than the walls or paint the moldings a contrasting color to the walls. If you have a chair rail (dado), paint that the same contrasting color. If you don't have a chair rail, make one with a stencil and paint, or use a wallpaper border.

Ugly. Some rooms have glaring architectural defects. They can be disguised by the clever use of wallpaper or paint. Consider covering badly scarred walls with mirror tiles, cork, wood flooring, or murals.

Your Favorite Things

Accessories give your room character and personality. They reflect your interests and hobbies. Through the use of accessories, you put your personal stamp on your room. Pictures, posters, sports equipment, flowers, shells, artwork — the list of accessories is endless. Your choice of accessories and the way you display them is limited only by your imagination.

Are you a collector? Place your coins, stamps or buttons in a display case and hang it in a prominent spot on the wall. Do you have a green thumb? Beautiful planters will make your plants look even better. Tennis, anyone? Yes, you can hang your racket.

TIP: Use your time wisely. Make your own braid rug while you're watching television. You can buy a braid rug kit, which will cost a lot less than buying the rug ready made.

Observe the usual elements of style when displaying your treasures:

If you're making a wall arrangement, give it some thought before you do anything. Choose a wall which will best set off your collection. Hang it at eye level so you and your friends can enjoy it.

If you're hanging several pieces, plan an interesting pattern.

Space correctly. Measure for accuracy.

Small objects should be grouped fairly closely or they'll "get lost" on a big wall.

Living plants should be placed where they will get enough sunlight. Don't put them close to a radiator or other heat source.

Don't overdo. Dozens of knick-knacks make a room look busy and confused.

TIP: If you're hanging something very light, like a poster, save the walls by using ordinary sewing needles rather than nails.

Creating Space and Privacy

Space is often at a premium, especially if you're sharing a room. Plan to make every inch count. Eliminate big, useless pieces. Look for pieces that perform several jobs. Here again, it helps to have a good imagination.

A sleeper sofa or murphy bed can be folded up during the day.

A storage trunk can double as a coffee table.

Build-it-yourself bookcases provide extra shelving.

Hide your jewelry, school supplies, or general junk in a plain cardboard box and cover it with pretty gift wrapping paper.

Take a critical look at your closet. Are you making the most of the space that you have? Additional rods are not difficult to install. Extra shelving can be built right in if your dresser isn't large enough.

Plan furniture placement to make the most of the space you have. A bed running lengthwise against a wall takes less space than one jutting out into the room. If you're sharing a room and both of you have a desk, try a "partner's desk" arrangement.

> **TIP:** Study the lines in *all* the elements in your room, that includes windows, doors, chairs, beds, and decorations. An interesting room has a mix of lines.

27

Room dividers provide privacy. The most common room dividers are screens, but you can also use two or three old doors hinged together or several sets of shutters joined together. Cover them with paint, wallpaper, fabric, posters, photographs — anything that strikes your fancy. If noise is a problem, try using cork. It soaks up sound.

TIP: Always talk to your roommate about any changes you're planning. She has rights too.

BIBLIOGRAPHY

Laura Ashley Bedrooms, Susan Irvine. Crown, New York.

"Look What You Can Do in One Weekend," Glamour. July 1988, pps. 202-204.

"Charmed Life," Glamour. August 1988, pps. 378-382.

Paint Magic, Jocasta Innes. Pantheon Books, New York.

"Decorating Workshop," Ladies' Home Journal. May 1988, pps. 142-145.

"A Designer's Private World," Seventeen. October 1986, pps. 154-159.

The Decorating Book, Mary Gilliatt. Pantheon Books, New York.

"Mario Does Windows," House Beautiful. June 1988, pps. 13-14.

"Our Best Small Apartment," House Beautiful. June 1988, pps. 54-63.

Designing with Flowers, Tricia Guild. Crown, New York.

Creative Decorating on a Budget. Better Homes and Gardens, New York.

The New Complete Basic Book of Home Decorating, edited by William E.
   Hague. Doubleday, New York.

Decorating Made Simple, Mary Jean Alexander. Doubleday, New York.

INDEX

DATE DUE			
T-6			

747.7
R

Rourke, Arlene C.

Decorating your
room.

797505 64786C 14895F